Man's Connection With The Various Planetary Bodies

Rudolf Steiner

THIS ARTICLE WAS EXTRACTED FROM THE BOOK:

Universe Earth and Man in their Relationship to Egyptian Myths and Modern Civilization

BY THIS AUTHOR:

Rudolf Steiner

ISBN 0766131378

READ MORE ABOUT THE BOOK AT OUR WEB SITE:

http://www.kessinger.net

OR ORDER THE COMPLETE BOOK FROM YOUR FAVORITE STORE

ISBN 0766131378

VIII.

Man's connection with the various planetary bodies. The earth's mission.

FOR the more exact understanding of our particular subject let us first consider the great world and then look down to the limited circle of our immediate earthly existence. We shall be able in this way to form a clear idea of what in Spiritual or Occult Science is understood in connection with the three conceptions we have brought together—Universe, Earth, and Man.

You will have already gathered from what has been said that in Spiritual Science one can by no means speak of the world as a mere material thing. We have seen how the manifold world-beings (we may not say world-bodies) that have been brought before you as the different embodiments of our earth—Saturn, Sun, and Moon—are quite other than mere material globes, each being, as we have seen, the dwelling-place of a host of spiritual beings, and created only according to the needs of the spiritual beings that live on them.

We saw how the sun separated from the earth because it had to be the home of certain highly exalted Beings who could only make use of the finer substances for their evolution, while man had to retain the other substances on the earth. Were we to investigate the whole wide world we should nowhere find anything that is material alone, everything is connected with a spiritual part. We have seen how the various earth-beings are connected with spiritual-beings. Stones and the minerals of the earth have their ego in that which surrounds us in the universe. Plants have their ego localised in the centre of the earth-planet, while their astral principle, which brings about the development of the flower, encircles them above the earth. Everything is pervaded by spirit, and thus our conception of a world-body is enlarged. We look up to some heavenly body and we know that it is but the expression of certain spiritual beings connected with a material planet.

Now, by developing certain capacities which are to be found slumbering within him, man is actually in a position to gain knowledge for himself regarding these bodies existing in space, and to-day we shall consider man in relation to the various planets.

We are surrounded on earth by minerals, plants, animals, and human beings, moreover we know that earthly affairs are regulated by higher beings who in Christian esotericism are described as Angels, Archangels, and Archai ; we also know that there are other beings concerned with the earth, even though they send their forces from the sun and the moon. To-day we have something to add to this. The question might rise in the mind of anyone : To what extent may one of the planets of our solar system be compared with another in respect to its inner nature?

To help us, let us consider the beings that visibly confront us in the present cycle of humanity, and enquire: How are the beings which surround us here as minerals, plants, animals, and men related to other beings in the universe? Of course we are dealing with this question from the standpoint of Spiritual Science, from knowledge gained through the development of clairvoyant consciousness; and of this development we shall speak later. In the first place let us ask: Are there on the other planets men such as those developing on our earth? Can clairvoyant consciousness discover such men? Clairvoyant consciousness answers: We do not find men on other planets in exactly the same form as upon earth, but we do discover that each planet, each heavenly body, has its particular mission. Nothing in the universe is repeated, other planets have other missions.

Our earth has originated from three preceding embodiments; the stage of existence we are now passing through (the human stage) has been passed through already by other beings; by Angels, for example, on the ancient Moon, by Archangels on the ancient Sun, and by Archai upon ancient Saturn. It is easy to make the mistake that these were men like ourselves, but we must bear in mind that on the ancient Moon there was no solid stone or mineral and therefore the beings who passed through their human stage there did so under entirely different conditions.

We know this, but we have to speak of it as the human stage. The Archangels, or Fire-Spirits, passed through their human stage in entirely different conditions, for the ancient Sun consisted only of warmth and gas, and beings passing through their human development there could not have bodies such as we have, with solid muscles, bones, etc. In earthly evolution nothing is repeated, every stage has its particular mission in the great household of cosmic existence.

Let us now consider for a time the evolution of our earth. If it is observed occultly we see it as a body inhabited by man on which he carries out his development. This development has only been made possible through the sun and the moon having separated from the earth, so that its forces were held in balance between the two. At the time when the earth was itself still sun (if we may call it so), it passed through an evolution in which it was incorporated with the sun. The sun was then itself at the planetary stage of existence, and was inhabited by Archangels, but because of advancing development it was possible for part of that which was embodied in it to rise to a higher existence at the cost of that other part which it sent forth as the earth-moon. In the great universe evolution proceeds in such a way that things which for a time have progressed side by side separate; the one expanding into higher regions, the other descending into a lower state. In order that certain beings might develop high enough the sun had itself to become a body fitted for their habitation; it advanced from planetary existence to fixed-star existence. We have to realize that a world-being like our sun has developed occultly from a planet to a sun. A sun is a planet that has progressed.

As was pointed out in the last lecture, after everything had united again, and the sun had once more at a certain period separated from the moon-plus-earth, man continued to dwell for a long period upon the earth, on into the present earth-period, without the spiritual Sun-Forces. Then through the advent of Christ the spiritual forces of the sun found again a place upon the earth. Now, if the Christ is embodied in the earth man must become more and more mature through receiving into him the Christ - Principle ; the material form of a planet depends on what it evolves in the way of beings.

Exactly in the same way as the sun evolved to its present exalted position, by withdrawing the finer substances because the Sun-being had need of them, so also will the earth. The substances of the earth will have then so changed as to be suited to man, or rather to what, in the distant future, will have developed from man and from the earth-beings he bears along with him ; for when man has become powerful he will draw other earth-beings along with him. What will happen then ? If man fills himself ever more and more with the Christ-Principle, if he absorbs more and more of the Sun-Forces which descended to earth with the Christ, he will himself grow ever more Christ-like, and will irradiate the whole heart with the Christ-Principle.

What is this Christ-Principle? Before we can know what it is we must know what the mission of the earth is, so that we can describe it by one special word. What is the mission of earthly existence? Let us ask first, What was the mission of the Moon's existence?

If we cast our clairvoyant vision back to the ancient Moon we find at the beginning, in the ancestors of all the beings on our earth, a very remarkable quality. These beings possessed a great deal, but one thing they lacked at the very beginning of the Moon period, and this thing we now find everywhere around us on our earth. The forces of the Moon, the predecessor of our earth, worked at first *unwisely*; the conditions on the Moon to begin with were such that nowhere could one have perceived an harmonious working together in *wisdom*. If one follows the evolution of the ancient Moon clairvoyantly one sees how the wisdom of the cosmos was gradually embodied in the beings who dwelt upon the Moon, by other beings who were round about it and who worked on it from without. Because of this the ancient Moon is called the Planet of Wisdom.

When the Moon period came to an end wisdom was in all things. Life on the Moon then went through an intermediate condition resembling a world-sleep called "pralaya," and when the beings again came forth from pralaya, and the earth appeared, they brought with them the wisdom with which they had been imbued on the ancient Moon. The consequence of this is that wisdom is implanted in all we observe around us. In all the creations which are the result of the Moon evolution, and which have a yet further mission, we find wisdom. Look where you will : take, for example, the leaf of any plant ; the more closely you observe it the more wonderful it appears, because the several parts are arranged according to the highest wisdom. Take a portion of the human thigh-bone ; there also the constituent parts are arranged according to the highest wisdom so as to form a support capable of carrying the upper part of the body.

No engineering skill of to-day can equal the bridge-building of this mighty wisdom. In all the other human organs, and indeed in all the surrounding world, we see wisdom at the root of everything. Man can only absorb this wisdom in a bungling way into his inner being on the earth. Microcosmic wisdom is something only to be learnt from the objects that surround man here. Wisdom is in all things, including those parts of man in which he does not consciously participate.

Following the course of history, we often extol human wisdom. How wonderful it seems to us when we learn that at a particular time man made this or that discovery. The art of paper making, for example, was discovered in recent times; it was an accomplishment of human intelligence—but wasps knew how to do it long before man. A wasps' nest, however, is not built by individual wasps, but by the group-soul of wasps ; it is built of exactly the same material as our paper. These group-souls possessed long ago something which human wisdom will only gain gradually. This wisdom, which is found deeply ingrained in everything that exists on earth, had to take form gradually, and we shall see how this was brought about throughout the Moon period ; how at that time wisdom warred against un-wisdom, and how the ancient Moon then bequeathed to the Earth the germs of beings in whom wisdom had been implanted.

What is to be implanted in a similar way in the beings of our Earth? Just as wisdom was implanted in our predecessors on the ancient Moon, so love has to be implanted on our planet. Our planet (the Earth) is the planet of love. The development of this, the first instilling of love, had to be in its lowest form. This happened during the Lemurian epoch, when the ego of man took shape ; at that time the development of love in its lowest form began through the separation of the sexes. All further development consists in the continual refinement, the spiritualizing, of this love-principle. Just as in the Moon-period wisdom was instilled into Moon-beings, so one day, when our earth shall have attained its goal, all earthly beings will be filled with love.

Let us now turn for a moment to the next planetary existence, that which is to succeed our Earth—the Jupiter planet. When the beings reappear who will inhabit Jupiter they will regard all those in their environment with their own spiritual powers of perception ; and just as with our intellect we admire the wisdom contained in stones, plants, and animals, and indeed in everything that surrounds us—just as we draw wisdom from them that we also may have it—the Jupiter-beings will direct their forces to all that surrounds them, and the love which had been implanted in them during the Earth evolution will be wafted to those who now surround them. In the same way that we analyse objects and learn from the wisdom contained in them, so the Jupiter-beings will edify themselves with the out-pourings of love that proceed from the beings about them. This love which is to develop on Earth can only develop through earthly egos being related one to another in the way described. Development in this direction can only take place through men being torn away from group-soul qualities; through one man drawing close to another; only thus can true love develop. Where egos are united within the group-soul there is no true love. Beings must be separated from each other so that love may be offered as a free gift. Only by such a separation as has come about in the human kingdom, where ego meets ego as independent individual, has love as a free gift become possible. This is why an increasing individualism and a uniting of separate individuals had to come about on earth.

Think of the various beings that are united within a group-soul; the group-soul directs them as to how they shall act. Can it be said that the heart loves the stomach? No, the heart is united to the stomach by the being within who holds them together. In the same way the several animals in a group are united one with the other within the group-soul nature, and what they have to do is regulated by the wise group-soul.

Only when the group-nature is overcome, and individual confronts individual ego, can the sympathy of love be offered as a free gift from one being to another.

Man could only be prepared for this mission gradually, and we see how he passes through a kind of preparatory school for love before he is fully individualized. We see how, before he possessed a complete ego of his own, he was gathered into groups that were related by blood by guiding beings, and the members of these groups loved each other because of the blood tie. This was a great time of preparation for humanity. We have already pointed out that at this stage love was not a free gift, but was directed by a remnant of the cosmic wisdom ; we have seen how Luciferic beings worked here and opposed with their strong liberating force everything that gathered mankind into families and peoples through the power of the blood ; these Luciferic beings strove to make man independent.

Thus man continued gradually to mature that he might eventually receive the highest potency of love—the Christ-Principle, which expressed its nature in the words, " He who does not forsake father, mother, son, and daughter, he who does not take up his cross and follow Me, is not worthy of Me." These words are not to be understood trivially, but in the sense that, through reception of the Christ-Principle the ancient blood-brotherhood had to assume a new form, a feeling of " belonging to each other " which, regardless of material foundations, must pass from soul to soul, from man to man. The Christ-Principle has given the impulse by which man can love man, and that through being Christ-ened human love may become more and more spiritual. Love will become more psychic and more spiritual, and through this man will also draw along with him the lower creations, and will thus transform the earth. In a far distant future he will transform the entire substance of the earth, and so mature the earth-body that it will be enabled to unite again with the sun. Christ as Spiritual Sun has given the impulse by which the earth and the sun can again be united in one body at a future day.

We have surveyed the course of the evolution of the world ; we have seen how the body of the sun first separated from the earth, and how the mighty Christ Impulse descended, and how the impulse was thereby given towards a reunion of earth and sun so that they might rise to higher stages of existence. We have also realized that the earth is to produce human beings who have this as their mission. Therefore, when we look around upon the human kingdom, and desire to learn about man, we can find him only on the earth, for only here are conditions produced for such men as exist to-day. You may now ask : How is it with the other kingdoms of the earth ? Let us consider the vegetable kingdom. When clairvoyant vision sweeps out into the universe and we investigate the other planets belonging to our system, we find in all those belonging to our sun a vegetable kingdom entirely corresponding to our own; so that in our vegetable kingdom we have something that in its systematic life is a part of our whole universe.

Our solar system is peopled by a vegetable creation, and were the whole matter to be considered occultly we should see that each planet is peopled also by its own kind of human beings. It is easy to perceive an inner relationship between plants and the sun, and how the life of the plant is intimately connected with the life of the sun. If this is the case it must also be connected with all the planets belonging to the solar system. When we allow our thoughts to sweep back to the condition of the earth when it was still a Sun-planet, we know that man consisted of physical and etheric body, that is, he was at the stage of a plant. Man at that time had the value of a plant; he was in the position in which the vegetable kingdom is now. This kingdom is composed of beings consisting of physical body and etheric body. These confront us in a way that moves us to say that they have remained true to the sun; even now they clearly reveal their relationship with the sun.

Let us consider the nature of a plant according to Rosicrucian wisdom. We see the plant fixed in the ground by its roots, that is, the organ which leads it towards the centre of the earth—to its ego; and we see how it turns its organs of reproduction to the sun and absorbs its chaste rays.

Let us now turn to man. It is not difficult to imagine man as a reversed plant. If we think of a plant exactly reversed in position we have a man ; his reproductive organs are turned to the centre of the earth, and his root towards space. The animal stands half-way between these. Hence one can say in a spiritual sense, when the soul-nature of the world passed through the various kingdoms it passed through a vegetable, an animal, and a human existence. Plato expresses this in a beautiful way. He says : " The world-soul is crucified on the cross of the world-body." Man has passed through the plant stage which directed him to the centre of the earth. The position of animals is expressed in the horizontal position of the spine. Man's position is that of the plant, only reversed. Thus the cross arose.

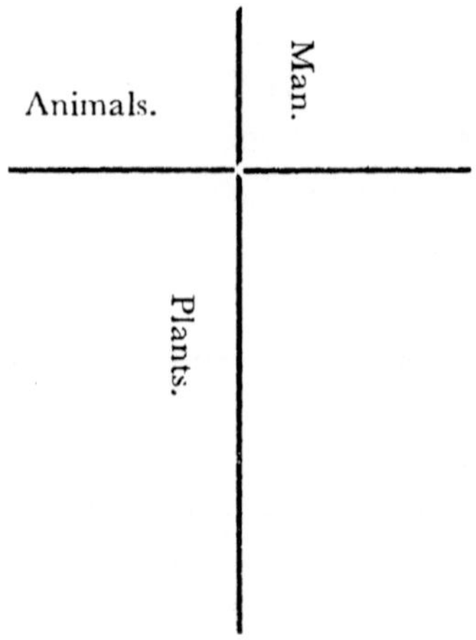

On it the world soul is crucified ; this is the profound esoteric meaning of the cross. In the plant of to-day we have a being which strives towards the sun, which has, in a certain sense, remained united with the sun, hence it has the opposite direction to man. Animal forms on the various planetary existences are partly alike and partly different; even here the animal stands midway between man and plant.

If we now pass to the mineral kingdom we find in the forms of crystals something that directs us into space far beyond our solar system. In the formative forces of the mineral kingdom we find forces which reach far beyond the solar system. We are led, especially when considering those forms of the mineral kingdom through which the light passes, to a perception of what takes place far beyond our solar system. The most abstract thing, and that which has least individual existence, yet forms at present the foundation of our life, is the mineral. It has a universal existence; the higher the being the more it is suited to the system of our earth and sun.

We will now consider this point with regard to man. If man were adapted to forces that ruled on the earth alone he would be condemned to exist only on the earth; he could never become a citizen of the universe; he could speak of nothing that takes place beyond the earth. Though he is adapted, through his outward form, to the conditions of the earth, he has also through his higher powers a part in all the higher beings who are connected with the earth. That which limits man to the earth has reference to his body alone; the spiritual powers with which he is furnished lead him far beyond the earth. Here again we have to distinguish between different forces. In order that we may understand them let us dwell first on those forces that can be easily classified.

We have in the first place the power which called up pictures before our spiritual eyes during the Atlantean epoch. Man's consciousness, to begin with, was a picture consciousness; only as evolution progressed was he gradually able to comprehend external objects by means of his objective consciousness. The consciousness which at the present time presents the sense world to us so that we see colours with our eyes, hear sounds with our ears, smell, and taste, was only differentiated at one time from out the general perception of warmth by the organ which was then like a kind of lantern — the pineal gland. Objective consciousness is purely of the earth. Wonderful as it may seem, all the sensations man is aware of, such as the colour of objects, resounding tones, have only existence on earth, and if we were to consider the beings of another planet we would find that at first we could not understand them. For instance, if we were to say something to these beings about the colour red they would not know what was meant; on their planet they have a different way of perceiving beings and things. What we call sense-perception applies only to our particular planet.

I have already explained that before sense-perception was differentiated it was inwardly connected with reproduction. Precisely as sense-perception is of the earth, so also is the form of reproduction (as it exists at present) of the earth, and is only adapted to this planetary existence : it exists for the purpose of providing the first foundation of that which is the mission of the earth, namely, love ; for love is to be developed upon the earth.

We now come to another human power. Suppose you observe some object ; as long as your eyes are turned to it you know that you are in correspondence with the object ; it acts upon you ; now turn your eyes away and hold the idea-picture of it in your memory ; the object has gone but the image remains. If man had not the capacity of retaining such images he would be an entirely different being, for as soon as his gaze left the object the image of it would also have disappeared, and in consequence he would not have power to connect the qualities of the things observed with his own qualities. That capacity of consciousness which makes the man of to-day able to retain the image of an object even when the object itself is gone, was his even on the ancient Moon ; it is the same capacity which then enabled him to see what was external to him in pictures. He could not at that time see outer objects as he does to-day, but when anything approached him an astral vision rose before him like a vivid dream-picture, but it was related in a particular way to the object he perceived.

Man's consciousness was then a picture consciousness, not an objective consciousness. Now he is in touch with the objects themselves ; the picture he sees *is* the object. A last remnant of picture consciousness has remained in our power to form memory-pictures. These are of greater value than the mere observation of external objects. In observing a number of objects that are similar to each other we bring them under one general idea. For instance, you have here so many pieces of chalk ; you group them under the general conception "chalk." In this way man rises to general conceptions for which no outer object exists. Man can work inwardly with his ideas, and if with this inward activity—with this power of ideation—he were to come in touch with beings outside our planetary existence he would be able, without having to refer to any object, to make himself more easily understood by them. Both the picture consciousness (which man possessed before he could perceive outer objects, and which was a dim clairvoyance) and also the *imaginative consciousness* which he will develop later are more far-reaching than mere sense observation.

When picture consciousness is acquired through occult development and man is able to perceive not only outer objects, but also, for instance. the human aura ; when in pictures he sees around him things of a soul and spirit nature ; when that which exists in the world rises before him in pictorial symbols, he has gained with his imaginative consciousness the power to connect himself with other things inhabiting other planets.

There is a yet higher degree of consciousness. This was possessed by man dimly during the Sun period, and to a slight extent he has it still —it is dreamless sleep-consciousness. Man is not without consciousness when asleep ; neither is a plant without consciousness ; its consciousness is the same as that of man in ordinary sleep. Sleep is only a lower degree of consciousness, when things escape man's attention and he does not observe them.

Through developing certain forces man can gain the power to perceive what is around him during the state of dreamless sleep. This is a higher state of consciousness than picture-consciousness ; it is the consciousness plants have, but in a sleeping form. If one rises to this consciousness but permeates it with one's ego in clear day-consciousness one has attained to the degree of inspiration or, in accult development, to *inspired consciousness*. This consciousness does not act merely by means of pictures. When something flows from the object and passes into the observer it is a tone-consciousness, and cannot be compared with picture-consciousness. The man who experiences it enters into a spiritual world of tone ; this is the consciousness described by Pythagoras as " the Harmony of the Spheres." The whole world then utters forth its nature, and when man is asleep at night and the astral body and ego are withdrawn from his physical and etheric bodies, the harmonies and melodies of cosmic music pervade his astral body. The astral body is then immersed in true spiritual existence, and from the music of the spheres it draws power by which to restore its exhausted forces. Man is plunged at night within the music of the spheres, and through the tones ringing within him he feels strengthened and refreshed anew when morning comes. When conscious of this he is Inspired, and is capable of perceiving all that is contained within the solar system.

Through his ordinary senses and the intellect associated with them man perceives only the things of the earth ; through Imagination he comes in touch with the various planets ; when he has attained to Inspiration he comes in contact with the solar system. This fact has always been known in certain circles. Goethe, who was an Initiate, knew it ; hence in the prologue to Faust, the scene of which is set in the spiritual world—in heaven—he represents the Angel as saying :

> " The sun intones his ancient song,
> 'Mid rival chant of brother spheres."

From this we see that he knew that the secrets of the solar system are expressed in tones, and that one who can raise himself to Inspiration can learn these secrets. Goethe did not write this by chance, as we can see, for he maintains the character. In the second part of Faust, when he takes us up into the spiritual world he says again very much the same thing :

> " Sounding loud to spirit ears,
> Lo! the new-born day appears."

Spirit ears are the ears of the clairvoyant, who is able to perceive the harmonies of the solar system. If you could perceive the Sun-Forces streaming down on to the bodies of plants as they grow (these bodies whose roots and leaves terminate in flowers bathed round by the astral body, into which stream the forces of the sun) ; if you could perceive these forces secretly entering the earth through the flower, you would perceive them as spiritual music—the music of the spheres. This can, however, only be heard by spiritual ears.

Spiritual sound enters into flowers, that is the secret of the development of plants, each separate flower is the expression of the tones which give it form, and give to the fruit its character. The sun-tones are caught up by the plant, and these rule within it as spirit.

You perhaps know how form can be imparted by sound in the material world ; you may remember the experiment of the Chladnic sound-forms. How dust scattered upon a disc assumes certain figures as the result of sound ; in these figures we have the expression of the sound that produces them. Just as physical sound is caught up, as it were, in this dust, so the spiritual sound of the sun is caught up and absorbed by flower and fruit. It is hidden mysteriously in the seed, and when a new plant grows from the seed it is the sun-tone it has absorbed that conjures forth its form.

Clairvoyant consciousness looks around upon the vegetable kingdom, and in the flowers which form the variegated carpet of the earth's surface it sees everywhere the reflection of sun-tones. What Goethe says is true, " The sun intones his ancient song," but it is also true that these sun-tones stream to earth, are absorbed by plants, and re-appear when new plants spring from the seed. For in the forms of plants is heard the sun-tones which re-echo into space the music of the spheres.

Herein we see how universe and earth, how fixed star and planet, are spiritually in touch with each other, and we learn not only to look at what is in our environment in the physical world, but we also gain an inkling of how those who partake of Inspiration ascend to the sun.

There is a still higher state of consciousness, which, in the true sense of the word, we call *Intuition*; through it man can creep within the very nature of things. This is more than inspirational consciousness; here a man sinks himself into beings, he identifies himself with them. This leads him still further. Where does inspirational consciousness lead him? It leads him to where he feels one with the earth planet, for the egos of the plants are in the centre of the earth. When he perceives the sun-tone he becomes one with the planetary being that dwells in the centre of the earth; he becomes one with his planet; he can also become one with all other beings. He then goes through experiences that reach far beyond our solar system; his vision is extended from system-consciousness to *cosmic-consciousness*—intuition carries him beyond the several solar systems.

Thus we see that in the mineral kingdom we have something which in a homogeneous form furnishes us with a basis that extends far beyond our ordinary existence. We see that the present human form is a physical earthly form, but that man will raise himself once more from ordinary earthly-consciousness to planetary-consciousness through imagination; to system-consciousness through inspiration; to cosmic-consciousness through intuition.

This is the path humanity has to travel in so far as it is connected with the entire evolution of the world. In the next lecture we shall descend from his study, which has led us outwards, to that which has taken place in more recent ages of earthly existence, in the Egyptian and Grecian ages, and in our own age. We shall see how the macrocosm, the mighty *universe* of which we have formed some idea to-day, is reflected in the life and conception of individual *man*—the microcosm.

Printed in the United States
127795LV00001B/95/A

9 781425 361358